I Could
Pee on This, Too

· · · · · · · · · · ·

AND MORE POEMS BY MORE CATS

I Could
Pee on This, Too

• • • • • • • • • •

AND MORE POEMS BY MORE CATS

BY FRANCESCO MARCIULIANO

CHRONICLE BOOKS
SAN FRANCISCO

Library of Congress Cataloging-in-Publication Data available.

ISBN 978-1-4521-3294-5

The following photos © copyright Photographer/Veer: Ivonne, 2 (two mice). The following photos © copyright Photographer/iStockphoto: luoman, 2 (typewriter); tomorca, 28; erlobrown, 51; SondraP, 54; fxegs, 102; WebSubstance, 105; darrial, 106. The following photos © copyright Photographer/Shutterstock: David Franklin, 36, 53, 74, 102 (polaroid stack); 501room, 20, 51, 62, 81 (picture frames); Stephen Rees, 3, 7, 11, 35, 61, 87 (folded paper); Peshkova, 28, 48, 73, 84, 96 (hanging frame); Kim Reinick, 31 (crumbs); Irtsya, 5, 16, 20, 25, 31, 41, 42, 47, 51, 53, 59, 62, 67, 68, 77, 78, 81, 89, 99, 105, 106, 110 (wallpaper pattern); Konrad Kaczmarzyk, 6, 12, 16, 20, 36, 54, 68, 74, 78, 81, 99, 100, 102, 106 (background texture); Studio DMM Photography, Designs & Art, 5, 12, 54, 68, 77, 106, 110 (photo corners); M.E. Mulder, 11, 35, 61, 87 (tape); Melissa King, 25, 99 (photo corners); Picsfive, 5 (notecard), 15, 92 (magnets); Africa Studio, 6, 73; mark cinotti, 10-11; FXQuadro, 12; Nailia Schwarz, 15, 25; Silberkorn, 15, 92 (refrigerator); Daria Trofimchenkova, 16; nednapa, 19 (planner); Courtney A Denning, 20; 9george, 22; ToskanalNC, 31; gvictoria, 32; sima, 34-35; Anna Sheveleva, 36; Winai Tepsuttinun, 39; Robert Red, 41; MaraZe, 42; scenery2, 42 (picture frame); Ailisa, 44; Alaskaphoto, 47; ziviani, 48; Linn Currie, 53; Lubava, 59; phloen, 60-61; photo_master2000, 62; Artur Synenko, 65; sarkao, 67; Magdanatka, 68; horvathta, 74; Renata Apanaviciene, 77; Tony Campbell, 78; Alena Ozerova, 81; vipman, 82; Masyle, 84; Tei Sinthip, 86; Rrrainbow, 89; IhorL, 91; MaxyM, 92; FabrikaSimf, 95; Velislava Todorova, 96; Lucky Business, 99; Schankz, 109; Okssi, 110. 5 © copyright Stacey Bell.

Manufactured in China

Designed by Hillary Caudle and Emily Dubin

10 9 8 7 6 5 4 3 2 1

Chronicle Books LLC
680 Second Street
San Francisco, California 94107
www.chroniclebooks.com

DEDICATED TO
Leelo and Kiki,
who eagerly await
their book royalties.

CONTENTS

· · · · · · ·》· · · · · ·

INTRODUCTION

· · · · · · ⟩≈ · · · · · ·

Ever since the first cat walked into an Ancient Egyptian's home, scratched his nose, demanded to be fed, and was proclaimed a god because who else could have such chutzpah, people have struggled to find out what is going on inside the feline mind.

Fortunately, the cats saw the desperation in our eyes—before looking right past us at a smudge on the wall—and gave us a rare, in-depth look into their hopes, dreams, and pointed critiques about our own lives with their very first collection of verse, *I Could Pee on This and Other Poems by Cats*. And so like any household is always improved with a second cat, we thought why not ask for a second volume of poetry? Unfortunately, though, the cats batted the book contract behind the fridge, along with their favorite toy, the bottle cap to every soda that went flat, and the keys to a car we haven't been able to drive for six weeks.

But the contract was found and the cat authors returned with more poems to offer even greater insight into what they want from us, what they want for themselves, and how they don't have time to hear what we want in return. Within these very pages you'll see the world as if through their eyes, understand the world as if through their minds, and taste the world as if you just grabbed someone else's slice of pizza off their plate with your teeth only to drop it sauce-side down on the good carpet.

Yes, for thousands of years the cat's internal thoughts have remained a mystery to us. But thanks to this book and the power of their poetry, you'll finally understand everything your cat is feeling, doing, saying, and outright dismissing no matter how many times you say "Why?' No!" or "I was going to wear that." Then you can keep treating them like a god, because otherwise your house keys are going behind the fridge, too.

OUR PEOPLE

·········≫━━▷·········

Everybody

Should have a cat (or two)

So that they can know true love

And know their true place

CAT CREDO

I Could Pee on This, Too

I could pee on this

    I could pee on this, too

I could hack up on this rug

    I could rework this carpet as well

I could shred the hell out of this ottoman

    Which would inspire me to do the same

    with this chair

I'm so glad now to be living

    With a fellow accomplished artist

Than just a human critic

    Whose every review is a withering

    "AUGH!"

I'm Sorry

. . . .

I'm sorry I knocked

That giant pot of pasta sauce

All over your kitchen

But in my defense

I've already forgotten why you're upset

Hey, are those floor meatballs for me?

I Watch

. . . .

I watch you sleep

I watch you eat

I watch you read

I watch you walk

I watch you in the shower

I watch you get dressed

I watch you from a distance

I watch you from behind a curtain

And I watch you knowing

If I were a human

I'd be in jail and not on your lap

A Name

· · · · · · · · ·

Patches

Smokey

Callie

Snickers

Luna

Misty

Schnoogles

Simba

Choosing a name is always hard

On the first day of adoption

But from now on it will be

"Princess Penelope PoofFace"

Even though your driver's license says

   "Steve"

Stone-Faced

. . . .

I'm not bored

I'm not aloof

I'm not disinterested

I'm not removed

I'm just trying really, really hard

To keep a straight face

As I watch the constant absurdity

That is your daily life

You Are the Last Person

. . . .

You are the last person

I would ever want to hurt

Twice

Today

So get your act together

And stop trying to take me off the bed

Why?

My eyes go dim

My limbs go slack

My mind goes blank

While you smile like a lunatic

While you press me to your face

While you take yet another selfie

And I take a moment to discover

A camera really can steal one's soul

Leave Me Alone

Leave me alone

It's Monday and I need to think

Leave me alone

It's Tuesday and I need to rest

Leave me alone

It's Wednesday and I need to stare

Leave me alone

It's Thursday and I need to yawn

Leave me alone

It's Friday and I need to stretch

WAKE UP! WAKE UP! WAKE UP!

It's Saturday at 3 am

And I need to celebrate the end of my
  workweek

Welcome New Cat

Welcome New Cat

Let me show you around

This is my couch

This is bed

These are my toys

That is my food

Over there is my kitchen

Hallway, Living Room, and Home Office

This is my human

And here is the door

Because as you can clearly see

There is nothing here for you

Special Bond

I see the dog follow you down the hall

I watch the dog follow you up the stairs

I look at the dog follow you in the
  bathroom

I notice how close you two are when you walk

I realize how far we two are when we sit

And I worry if I'm missing out

And I wonder if we should have that bond

And I recall how you can go on for hours
  on end

About some rude cashier from two days ago

And I welcome our time apart

Fish

· · · · ·

I'VE GOT YOU NOW, FISH!

I'VE GOT YOU NOW, FISH!

I'VE GOT YOU NOW, FISH!

But the fish is not flinching

And the water is not wet

And this is a game on your tablet, isn't it?

So you have a good laugh

So you film me looking like an idiot

So you better have two of these tablets

Because I just found the app for

   "Scratching Post"

You Believe in Me

. . . .

You believe

I want to be taught a trick

You believe

I want to learn my name

You believe

I will one day learn the meaning of
   the word "No"

You believe

That when I sneeze and you say, "God
   bless you"

Maybe this time I'll say, "Thank you"

Because you believe in me

Possession

I'm sorry

But I didn't realize

That after the life we've built together

After everything we've shared

After I've given you my world

You still see us

In terms of what is yours

What is mine

And whatever is placed between two slices
   of bread

Is suddenly not just anyone's for the taking

Gratitude

I can't thank you enough
For everything you've done for me
Apparently
Because you can't stop asking
For another show of affection

Concern

. . . .

If you think I'm apathetic

If you think I'm too distant

If you think you're not my concern

Just know

I saw you smash your toe three weeks ago

And I've now come over to see how you are

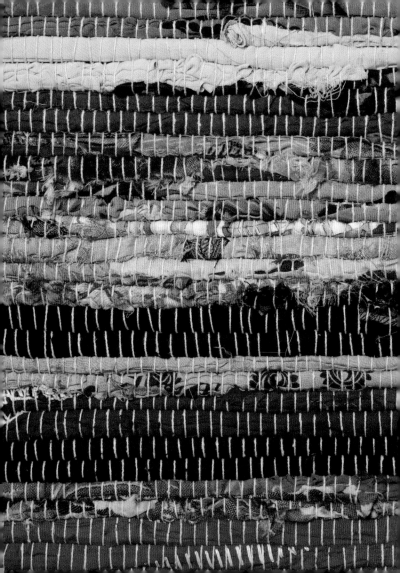

OUR HOME

.... ⊰ ....

Home is where the heart is

And two people are

And another cat is

And I see three things I can do without already

CAT CONVICTION

Sit

. . . .

You need this piece of paper?

Here, let me sit on it

You need to write in this notepad?

I think I'll sit on it

You want to read this magazine?

Oh, I will sit on this

You hope to use your laptop?

I'll fall asleep across your keyboard

Until my drool shorts out your shift key

Because when I control the means of

   communication

I control your world

NAILS

. . . .

Nails

Nails!

NAILS! NAILS! NAILS!

Do not brakes make

Which is why you just saw me skid sideways

Across your hardwood floor

And through the open door to your basement

You Also Live Here

. . . .

It's come to my attention
That you also live here
Which makes all that cleaning you do
Far less thoughtful

I Get Along

. . . .

I get along with you
I get along with your family
I get along with everyone I ever meet
Only to get to hear someone say,
"I don't know why you got a cat
They're so unfriendly."
I get the urge sometimes
To wield my claws on the whole world

Dinner

· · · · · · · ·

Judging by your wide eyes

Judging by your gaping mouth

And judging by the fact

You keep smacking me on the head

I must be eating your food,

Fellow cat

But if it's any consolation

My food was delicious, too

So clearly our person isn't playing any

   favorites

Assassin

When I kill a bug

You thank me

When I kill a mouse

You thank me

So when I kill your plants

Instead of shouting

"My orchids! My prize-winning orchids!"

Say, "Thank you

For killing them before they kill us"

Because I know what I am doing

And heads up, I don't really trust your bird

All for You

· · · · · · · · · · · ·

You read more

You go out more

You talk to loved ones more than ever

Yes, since I did you the favor

Of knocking your flatscreen to the floor

Your life has become so fulfilling

That the only thing holding you back is

   sleep

So let me show you what I did to your sheets

The Box

. . . .

The box is a toy

The box is a bed

The box is a hiding space

The box is a home

The box didn't mean a damn thing to me

Until the other cat claimed it

The box is now my fortress

That I will defend to the bitter end

Splash

. . . .

Splash

Splatter

Slosh

Tip spill flood

And yet again

I show the water dish who's boss

And you who's bored

To Fly

. . . .

To fly

To soar

Perchance to reach that top shelf

Perchance to land somewhere near that
  top shelf

Perchance not to miss that top shelf

By a good fifteen feet

Perchance not to plummet like a hairy rock

On to the wedding china

To run

To hide

Perchance to wait behind the drapes

Until you blame the other cat

Little Hat

. . . .

If you make me wear

A little hat

You might as well get me

A little shirt

And little pants

And the deed to your property

Because dressing as a human

Is when the pigs in "Animal Farm"

Took control of everything

I'm Here for You

I know that shrug

I know that "I'm fine"

I know all the things you say and do

When you're feeling unwanted

Unknown

Unseen

But I'm here for you

But I'm listening to you

But I'm staring at the wall for six hours
  straight

Looking at you

Ghost

So maybe you can moan to the homeowners

About how it was you who broke their lamp

And show that you're here for me, too

Welcome Back

. . . .

After being all alone

After being all over this house

After being bored all day long

You return with a smile

You bend down to give me a hug

You watch me evade your big arms

And lick the plastic bags you got from the
  supermarket

Until it's tomorrow and I can finally be
  alone again

Home Decor

· · · · · · · · · · · · ·

Nudge nudge nudge

Then you grab the vase

Before I can shove it off the shelf

Nudge nudge nudge

Then you grab the lamp

Before I can shove it off the table

Nudge nudge nudge

Then you grab the objet d'art

Before I can shove it off to its rightful doom

Every time I start to nudge something

You quickly grab it and put it away

Where it can never be seen again

And that's how I help you get rid of

All the ungodly mistakes you call home decor

Canary

· · · · · · · ·

I want the canary in that cage

I want the canary in that cage

I want the canary in that cage

OH DEAR LORD

CAN THAT BIRD FIGHT BACK!

I MEAN OW OW OW HOLY HELL!

OW!!!

Sigh

I want the cheese on that plate...

OUR THOUGHTS

There is a word

We cats have

When we want to say "Thank you."

But none of us can remember it

CAT CONFESSION

I Don't Like

I don't like the cat carrier

I don't like being put in a box

That isn't my own choosing

I don't like the cat carrier

I don't like being taken someplace

That I can't walk away from

I don't like the cat carrier

Because it means I don't have a say

Until you reach in and I rip your hands

   to shreds

Self-Confidence

I bet I'm stunning

I bet I'm gorgeous

I bet I'm the most ravishing

Eye-catching

Outright bewitching

Feline there has ever been

Far better than any other in this house

And nothing like that hot mess of a cat

I always see in the bathroom mirror

The Day My Head Got Stuck in a Plastic Cup

. . . .

The day my head got stuck in a plastic cup

Was a wake-up call for me

To learn, not just live

To excel, not just exist

To want better, not just want

To get my act together

And in that very act

Reclaim my self-worth

The second day my head got stuck in a
   plastic cup

I decided I'd rather embrace my flaws

Flashback

. . . .

If I could go

Back in time

And give just one warning

To my younger self

It would be

Never, ever try catnip

Because I actually thought

I did go back in time

Only to find out I was warning the toaster

Humans

Humans

You have a great capacity for love

You have a great desire to resolve

You could be such a remarkable species

You just need some motivation

You just need a little inspiration

You just need to get off this damn couch

Which is why I've claimed the entire living
  room sectional

Now go out into the world and make me proud

Cuddling

Whenever I cuddle

With the other cat

I think, "It's only a matter of time

Before one of us bites the other."

"It's only a matter of time

Before this just ends in biting."

"It's only a matter of time

Before one of us gets bit."

So I bite the other cat

Because I'd rather prove you can't avoid
  destiny

Than show I can't see what's coming

I Bonk

I bonk you on the forehead

I bump you on the nose

I bash you in the chin

To show that I love you

To say that you are mine

To scent mark your entire face

So when the new cat and I

Realize we can't make it work

I'm the one who gets to takes you

To whatever place you get next

I Can Just Tell

I can just tell

By your very light touch

By your very gentle stroke

By your very soft hands

As you pet my very happy head

That you are a very nice person

Who's never done a hard day's labor in
   your life

The Moment

. . . .

The moment you put

Your foot in your shoe

And realized what I had done

Was the moment I realized

My vomit in your other 15 shoes

Would prove anticlimactic

I See a Glint of Light

I see a glint of light

I see a gleam upon the wall

I see the world but in a moment

I dare not look away

My eyes grow wide with wonder

My heart grows strong with hope

My mind grows wings and lifts me high

My life is born anew

I am one with all the universe

I am one with all of you

I am all I cherish, all I dream

I am all that we can be

Then suddenly that glint of the light

That gleam upon the wall

That pure moment fades away

And I go take a nap or cough up a hairball
  or whatever

You Are Way Too

You are way too loud

You are way too big

You are way too messy

You are way too smelly

You are way too far removed

From the refined demeanor

Our person clearly expects

From two cats

Named "Nummers" and "Bobo"

Sleeping My Life Away

If there's one thing I've learned

In all my years

Sleeping my life away

It's that when I wake up

Everyone is in bed

And I'm clearly not missing anything at all

Laundry

I bury myself deep
In your laundry basket
Because sometimes I pretend
This place is a prison
This basket my means of escape
And you the cruel, cruel warden
Who switched my food without warning

There's a Toy on My Head

There's a toy on my head

You know there's a toy on my head

You placed the toy on my head

You're taking pictures of the toy on my head

You're laughing

There's now an idea in my head

You put that idea in my head

Soon you won't be laughing at all

I guess this is how every revolution starts

One poorly placed cloth octopus at a time

Clear Picture

Whenever I think of you

I have such a clear picture

Such a vivid image

Of your kind eyes

Of your warm smile

Of your loving presence

That I probably don't need

To actually look at you

For another month or so

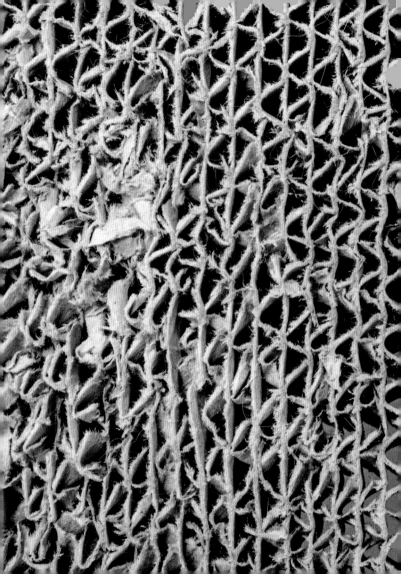

OUR RULES

The first eight lives

Are for practice

The ninth is for revenge

CAT CODE OF CONDUCT

Hello?

. . . .

Hello? Hello?

Are you talking to me?

I heard you from the other room

I see you're on the phone

I don't have my own phone

So you should talk directly to me

You should pay attention only to me

You should notice how dark it got

When I just pushed the lamp off your table

You should put down the phone now

So we can talk about that mess

Personality

Life is divided into

Extroverts

Introverts

And those who split the difference

By lying across your face

And then not responding to your muffled

   small talk

High Cost of Living

Yes

I did eat

The twenty you left on the counter

And I appreciate your anger

And I appreciate your distress

But mostly I appreciate

That you forgot there were two fifties

  along with it

Season to Taste

· · · · · · · · · · · · · · · ·

Parsley

Sage

Rosemary

Thyme

Cat hair

Cat hair

Cat hair

Are the basic ingredients

Of any kitchen

With low counters

For the Holidays

. . . .

For the holidays
I just want your love
I just want your kindness
I just want your constant
Companionship in my life
For the holidays
I just want your warmth
I just want your kisses
I just want you always
Lying by my side at night

For the holidays

I just want your understanding

I just want your forgiveness

I just want the first four things

Sung in the "12 Days of Christmas"

Because they all sound delicious

Oh, and get the five golden rings, too

So I have something to knock under the fridge

My Replacement?

When my family brought home

The adorable new kitten

I thought

"Oh no! They think my time is over!

"Oh no! They're prepping my replacement!

"Oh no! They moved on from me already!"

But then I saw the new kitten get stuck

In a wine rack and a shoe rack

At the same time

And thought,

"Oh. No.

"They just want to give this old cat a great
   big laugh."

So Many, Many Jobs

You're my kitchen staff

My sanitation crew

My nail salon

My spa attendant

My hair stylist

Even my dental technician

You handle so many, many jobs

Throughout my every day

That I have every confidence you'll be great

In your new position as my scratching post

When you sleep

18 hours a day

You only have so much time

To plan your day

To achieve your goals

To live your dreams

Which is why when I greet you

It's always butt-first

So my eyes are free to see what needs to

get done

Yes, Sometimes

Yes

Sometimes I belch

Yes

Sometimes I pass gas

Yes

Sometimes something gets hacked up

And yes

Sometimes I do all three at once

Because yes

I'm just that comfortable

With you

With myself

And with anyone you might ever invite over

Might as Well Ask

. . . .

Why did I just walk up

And suddenly smack the other cat

For seemingly no reason at all?

You might as well ask

Why do birds sing

Why do cows moo

Why do ferrets ferret

And why I would

Smack them all upside the head today, too

It's called being in a mood, okay?

Birthday

Every birthday

It's the same thing

You make a big deal

You make me wear a hat

You make a birthday cake

I knock the cake on the floor

And you make like you

Don't still have a bunch of gifts you
  can open

Windfall

· · · · · · · · · · ·

Three Hundred

Forty

Eight

Dollars

And twenty-two cents

All in your loose change

All batted off of your table

All by me over all these years

Because saving is a lot easier than

   people think

Prey

· · · · · ·

Yes, I play with my prey

Yes, I test its skills

Yes, that's considered cruel

Yes, that's considered brutal

But no, a scientific magazine

Won't publish my studies

If all I write is "Yum."

Real Close

. . . .

If you listen very carefully

If you bend down very close

If you wait until the very moment

I ram my nose up another cat's butt

You will hear muffled laughter

Because even I can't believe

This is how we all decided to tell each
  other "Hello!"

Roommates

. . . .

When we first met, fellow cat

I did not care for you

I did not know why you were here

But then we became friends

And then we tried to be more than friends

Until we realized our person had us fixed

And so we are apart

And we moved to opposite sides of the house

But now when we pass

Each other in the hall

We each give a little nod

And we each give a little smile

As we each remember the time

We both jumped on our person's lap

When he was still naked right after his
    shower

ACKNOWLEDGMENTS

This book would not be possible without the incredible support of my family and loved ones. And cats. And the support of my friends. And more cats. And the support of all the great cat fans. And their cats. In short, I owe a lot of cats dinner.

FRANCESCO MARCIULIANO is the author of the bestselling books *I Could Pee on This*, *I Could Chew on This*, *I Knead My Mommy*, and *You Need More Sleep*. He writes the internationally syndicated comic strip *Sally Forth* and the webcomic *Medium Large*. He was head writer for the Emmy award–winning children's series *SeeMore's Playhouse* and has written for Smosh and the Onion News Network. He is on Twitter at @fmarciuliano.